The INSIDE & OUT *GUIDE to*

INVENTIONS

CHRIS OXLADE

THE INSIDE & OUT GUIDE TO INVENTIONS
was produced by

David West 옷옷 Children's Books
7 Princeton Court
55 Felsham Road
London SW15 1AZ

Designer: Rob Shone
Illustrator: Moorhen Studios
Editor: Dominique Crowley
Picture Research: Victoria Cook

First published in the United States in 2006 by
Heinemann Library
a division of Reed Elsevier Inc.
Chicago, Illinois

Customer Service 888-454-2279
Visit our website at www.heinemannlibrary.com

11 10 09 08 07 06
10 9 8 7 6 5 4 3 2 1

ISBN-13: 978-1-4034-9085-8 (library binding - hardcover)
ISBN-10: 1-4034-9085-6
ISBN-13: 978-1-4034-9092-6 (pbk.)
ISBN-10: 1-4034-9092-9

A full reference is available from the Library of Congress.

Acknowledgements
The author and publisher are grateful to the following for permission to reproduce copyright material:
Pages 12t & b, 15m – NASA; 16t, 21t, 25t – Library of Congress; 6t – Thameside Local Studies and Archives; 9t – Mercedes Benz Classic; 14t – Ray Hooley, oldengine.org; 15t – Western Front Association; 17t – reproduced courtesy of Museum Victoria; 18t – Science Museum, Science & Society Picture Library; 19b – Hong Kong Graphics and Printing; 23t – Marcus Kaar, portraitkaar.at; 24t – John Jenkins, sparkmuseum.com; 24b – David Wort; 26b – Sony United Kingdom Ltd.; 27t – NMPFT, Science & Society Picture Library; 29t – Dr. Ing Horst Zuse

Every effort has been made to contact copyright holders of any material reproduced in this book. Any omissions will be rectified in subsequent printings if notice is given to the publishers.

Printed and bound in China

The INSIDE & OUT GUIDE to
INVENTIONS

CHRIS OXLADE

Heinemann Library
Chicago, Illinois,

CONTENTS

INTRODUCTION

AN INVENTION IS A NEW MACHINE, A NEW TOOL, OR A new way of doing something. Over thousands of years inventions have changed the way we live. They help us to work, travel, and manufacture things. Inventions entertain us, help us grow food, and enable us to find out about our world. Some inventions come from a flash of inspiration, when an inventor has an idea. But most are the result of many years of hard work.

STEAM ENGINE

STEAM PROVIDED THE POWER FOR the very first type of engine. At first these simply pumped flood water from mines. Inventors put steam engines on wheels, and the steam locomotive was born.

NEWCOMEN'S ENGINE
In 1712, Thomas Newcomen built his first beam engine. The piston moved one end of the beam. The other end operated a water pump.

Early steam engines did not move. They were too big and heavy to drive locomotives. Lighter, more powerful steam engines were developed in the early 1800s, and soon the first steam locomotives appeared. The *Rocket* (right) was built in 1829 by British engineers George Stephenson (1781–1848) and his son Robert (1803–1859). *Rocket* won the Rainhill Trials, a competition held to find a locomotive to pull trains on the new Liverpool and Manchester Railway in northern England. *Rocket* won because it had a multi-tube boiler. This invention allowed *Rocket* to make steam faster than its rivals.

Water barrel

Tender

TREVITHICK'S LOCOMOTIVE
British engineer Richard Trevithick (1771–1833) built high-pressure steam engines for pumping water from mines. In 1804 he put one of his engines on wheels, making the world's first steam locomotive.

STEPHENSON'S ROCKET
DURING THE RAINHILL
TRIALS, ROCKET REACHED
A SPEED OF 29 MPH. THIS
WAS A WORLD-RECORD
SPEED AT THE TIME.

Robert Stephenson (1803–1859)
was a British engineer. As well
as designing the Rocket with
his father, he was the chief
engineer for the London to
Birmingham railroad.

FIREBOX

Burning coal or wood in the firebox made hot gases that flowed into the boiler tubes. Fuel was stored in a box called the tender.

CYLINDERS

Steam from the boiler was fed to the cylinders. The steam pushed the piston out and then back in again to turn the drive wheel.

STEAM **EXHAUST** OUTLET

Exhaust steam from the cylinders was fed into the smoke stack. This flow of steam helped to pull heat from the firebox through the boiler tubes, heating the water.

Smoke stack

Fuel

Boiler

Steam valve

Boiler tubes

BOILER

Water in the boiler was heated by hot gases from the fire flowing along the boiler tubes. The heat turned the water to steam.

Drive wheel

7

AUTOMOBILE

THE FIRST EXPERIMENTAL AUTOMOBILES appeared on the roads in the 1880s. This was the start of a transportation revolution. Twenty years later, a huge motor industry was up and running. Cars were produced in their thousands.

The automobile became possible when the **internal combustion engine** was invented. The first engines were not powerful enough to move a car. But in the 1880s, German engineer Gottlieb Daimler (1834–1900) invented a small, lightweight, four-stroke **gasoline engine**. Daimler built his first car in 1887. Cars were rare until **mass production** began. Small, cheap cars, such as the Ford Model-T (right), then became available.

BENZ MACHINE
This is a Benz car from 1888. It has three wheels because it was based around a horse-drawn carriage. This is why early cars were known as "horseless carriages."

Headlight

Radiator

ENGINE
The Model-T had a four-cylinder gasoline engine. It could produce about 20 horsepower.

Starter handle

FORD PRODUCTION LINE
Henry Ford (1863–1947) was a pioneer of mass production. He designed the Model-T to be made cheaply on a production line. Until then cars had been made one by one.

GEARBOX
The Model-T had three **gears**. There were two forward gears and one reverse gear. The driver selected the gears with foot pedals.

BETWEEN 1908 AND 1927, THE FORD MOTOR COMPANY BUILT MORE THAN 15 MILLION MODEL-TS.

making gas-powered engines. In 1885 he converted an engine that ran on gases to run on gasoline. It powered the world's first car. Benz had made and sold more than 2,000 cars by 1900.

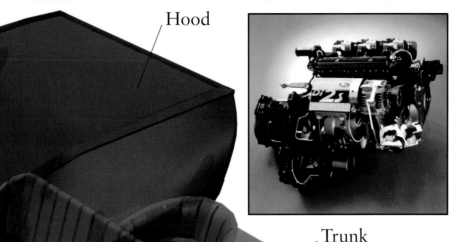

Hood

Trunk

Fuel tank

Rear axle

Brakes

Pneumatic tire

Running board

TWO AND FOUR STROKES

In a four-stroke engine, each cylinder fires on every other downstroke. In a two-stroke engine (left), it fires on every downstroke. Four-stroke engines are more efficient.

SUSPENSION

The Model-T had one suspension spring on the front axle and one on the rear axle. The wooden wheels had **pneumatic** tires.

CHASSIS

Like all early cars, the Model-T had a strong frame called a chassis. All the other parts of the car, such as the engine, body, and fuel tank, were bolted to the chassis.

BODYWORK

The body was made from metal panels bolted to the chassis. The fold-down fabric hood was raised in rainy weather.

BLACK GOLD

In the 1800s oil was known as "black gold" because it made people rich. Without the supplies of gasoline, made from oil, the automobile industry might have failed.

PLANE

MANY UNLUCKY INVENTORS WERE INJURED OR KILLED TRYING to fly with strap-on wings. It was not until the 1800s that the science of flight was understood. Aviators developed wings and invented ways of steering aircraft through the air.

LILIENTHAL GLIDES

Otto Lilienthal (1848–96) studied bird flight before building a series of gliders in the 1890s. He made more than 2,000 flights before he was killed in a crash.

One of the first planes to fly was a simple glider built in 1849 by British engineer Sir George Cayley (1773–1857). At the time there was no engine light enough to lift a plane into the air. The Wright brothers built their own gasoline engine for their famous *Flyer*, which made the first-ever controlled, powered flight in 1903. A modern, state-of-the-art plane, such as the F-35B strike fighter (right), uses many of the inventions developed since the first planes flew. These include the autopilot, the jet engine, radar, and vertical flight—where a plane can move up and down in the air without needing to move forward.

Stabilator

Fuel tank

RUSSIAN GIANT

Many modern planes, such as the giant Antonov An-225 cargo plane, are powered by a type of jet engine called a turbofan. The jet engine was invented by British Royal Air Force officer Frank Whittle in the 1930s.

EXHAUST NOZZLE

Exhaust from the engine comes out here, pushing the aircraft forward. The nozzle is swiveled to point downward for vertical flight.

F-35B STRIKE FIGHTER
THE F-35B IS A
"STEALTHY" AIRCRAFT.
ITS SHAPE MAKES IT
ALMOST INVISIBLE TO
ENEMY RADAR SYSTEMS.

Orville Wright (1871–1948) and Wilbur Wright (1867–1912) made hundreds of test flights with kites and gliders before building Flyer.

STABILIZING NOZZLES

During vertical flight, a nozzle under each wing blows engine exhaust gases downward. The flow of the gases is carefully controlled to keep the aircraft stable.

Rudder

Folded undercarriage

Fuel tank

Weapons bay

Gun

LIFT FAN

The F-35B is a short takeoff and vertical landing (STOVL) aircraft. The **thrust** for vertical flight is produced by a fan that is covered by doors during normal forward flight.

COCKPIT

A mass of electronic equipment helps the pilot fly, **navigate**, and use the F-35B's weapons. The pilot can see information about the plane's systems on a computer screen inside his helmet.

Avionics

Radar

ENGINE

Power comes from a single jet engine. The engine pushes the aircraft forward in normal flight and drives the lift fan and stabilizing nozzles in vertical flight.

Air intake

ROCKET

FIREWORK ROCKETS
A firework is a solid-fueled rocket. Inside is a powder that burns, making gases that shoot the rocket into the air. The rocket explodes when the fuel runs out.

A thousand years ago, the Chinese used rockets as weapons and as fireworks. These rockets used gunpowder as fuel. A rocket with solid fuel, such as gunpowder, is called a solid-fueled rocket. All rockets were solid-fueled until American rocket pioneer Robert Goddard (1882–1945) invented the liquid-fueled rocket. This design contains liquid fuel and a supply of **liquid oxygen**. The two liquids burn when they mix together. A liquid-fueled rocket is easy to control because the flow of fuel can be altered. Goddard launched his first rocket in 1926. His invention led to the development of the V2 rocket, a weapon used in World War II. Liquid-fueled rockets reached space in the 1950s.

FUEL

The V2 had two fuel tanks. One contained a mixture of **ethyl alcohol** and water, and the other had liquid oxygen. With the maximum amount of fuel on board, the rocket's range was 199 miles.

Ethyl alcohol and water tank

WARHEAD

The V2 could carry a ton of high explosive to its target. The explosive was detonated by a trigger when the nose hit the ground.

GUIDANCE SYSTEM

A guidance system kept the rocket on course. It used **gyroscopes** to detect changes in direction and control the rear vanes.

Fuse

THE GERMANS USED THE V2 TO BOMB ENEMY CITIES. MORE THAN 3,600 V2S WERE LAUNCHED BETWEEN 1944 AND 1945.

developed the V2 rocket in Germany in the 1930s and 1940s. After World War II he moved to the U.S., where he worked on long-range military rockets and space rockets.

STABILIZERS

Four stabilizing fins kept the rocket flying straight. There were two small control vanes on each fin. These were turned from side to side by the guidance system to make small adjustments to the direction of flight.

ENGINE

Fuel and liquid oxygen were pumped into the **combustion** chamber through 18 nozzles. They mixed in the combustion chamber, where the fuel burned, creating hot gases that rushed out of the exhaust nozzle. This stream of gas pushed the rocket forward.

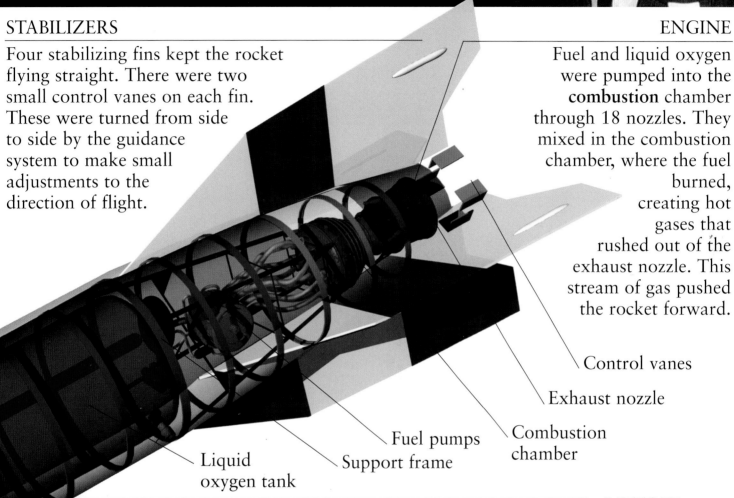

Control vanes

Exhaust nozzle

Combustion chamber

Fuel pumps

Support frame

Liquid oxygen tank

LIFTOFF

A space shuttle orbiter has three liquid-fueled rocket motors. The fuel is stored in the giant tank underneath the orbiter. The shuttle needs an extra push for takeoff, which comes from two solid-fuel boosters.

TANK

This new fighting machine, with its squealing tracks, heavy machine guns, and thick heavy armor, must have been a terrifying sight on the muddy battlefields.

The first tracked vehicles were developed in the early 1900s. They were used as farm tractors. At the beginning of World War I, Ernest Swinton (see page 15) had the idea of a tracked fighting machine. It would be able to drive through muddy fields, break through barbed wire defenses, and cross trenches. This would clear a path for troops. The first British tank was tested in 1915. A year later the Mark I tank went into battle. Early tanks often broke down or got stuck in mud, but by World War II, the tank was an important weapon.

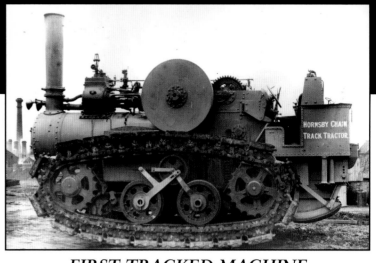

FIRST TRACKED MACHINE
*The 1905 Hornsby chain tractor was the first **self-propelled**, tracked vehicle. The tracks spread its 10-ton weight over the ground, stopping it from sinking into the mud.*

TRACKS

Each track was made of metal links (called shoes) joined together to make a continuous loop.

MODERN TANK UNITS
The tank is vital to a modern army. Tank units attack enemy tanks and support infantry. An advanced electronics system makes a tank's gun very accurate.

Drive chain   Gears

DRIVE WHEEL

A large rear wheel on each side drove the tracks round. Teeth on the wheel interlocked with holes in the track.

MARK I TANK
TANKS GOT THEIR NAME BECAUSE PEOPLE BUILDING THEM THOUGHT THAT THEY WERE MAKING WATER TANKS.

Ernest Swinton (1864–1951) was a British army officer. He realized that a tracked fighting machine could break the stalemate of trench warfare. His idea was put into practice in 1916.

SHUTTLE MOVER
Giant tracked vehicles called crawler-transporters carry space shuttles to their launch pad. Each one has eight enormous tracks.

ARMOR PLATING
The Mark I had side, roof, and front armor to protect against machine-gun fire. This was made up of steel plates about 0.5 inch thick.

Exhaust   Pistol ports

STEERING
The driver steered left and right by braking on one track or the other.

Front machine gun

Front wheel

Command post

Fuel tank

ARMAMENT
This Mark I tank was armed with six machine guns. Other models had two artillery guns and four machine guns.

Idler wheels

ENGINE
The tank was driven along by a huge Rolls Royce 105-horsepower engine. But because the tank weighed 28 tons, its top speed was only 4 mph.

FARM MACHINERY

THREE HUNDRED YEARS ago, farming was done by hand. Today machines, such as tractors, seed drills, and combine harvesters, plow fields, sow seeds, and harvest crops with great speed.

HORSE POWER
Combine harvesters were developed before mechanical tractors were invented. The first combines were hauled by teams of dozens of horses.

Air-conditioned cab

Reel

Harvesting a crop means reaping (cutting the stalks), threshing (knocking the seeds from the stalks), and winnowing (separating the seed from the straw and chaff). The first threshing machine was invented in 1786, and the first successful reaping machine in 1851. In the 1880s Hugh Victor McKay (see page 17) combined a reaping machine, threshing machine, and winnowing machine to make the first-ever combine harvester.

CUTTER
The reel pushes the crop against the cutter bar, where blades like scissors slice it off.

HARVEST TIME
At harvest time, combines move into the fields. They remove the grain from crops, such as wheat and corn. They store the grain and dispose of the straw and chaff.

operating a winnowing machine on his father's farm in Australia when the idea of a combine harvester came to him. He was just 17 at the time. He called his new machine the Sunshine Harvester.

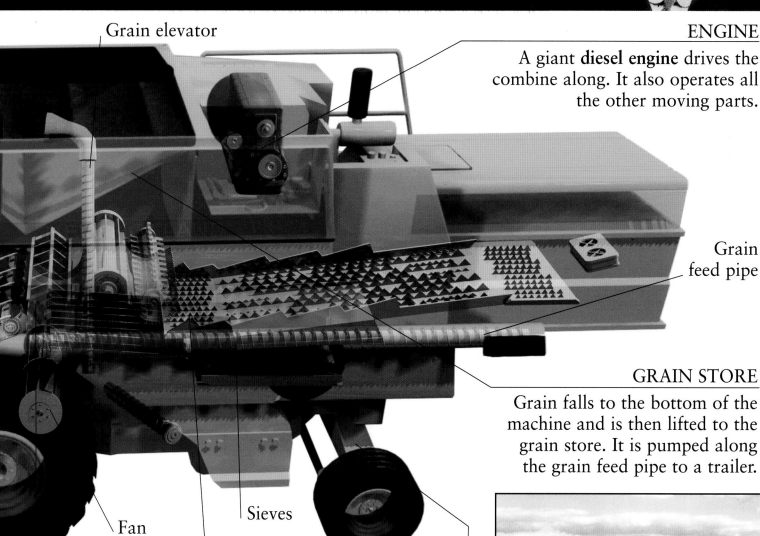

Grain elevator

ENGINE
A giant **diesel engine** drives the combine along. It also operates all the other moving parts.

Grain feed pipe

GRAIN STORE
Grain falls to the bottom of the machine and is then lifted to the grain store. It is pumped along the grain feed pipe to a trailer.

Fan

Sieves

AUTO-LEVELING AXLE
The rear axle tilts from side to side to keep the combine harvester level. This stops the grain from sliding to one side.

THRESHING CYLINDER
The cut crop is carried up to the threshing cylinder by a moving belt. Here it is squeezed and beaten to knock off the grain. Most grain falls through sieves.

STRAW WALKERS
The straw moves along vibrating plates, which allow any remaining grain to fall through. Underneath, a fan blows the chaff from the grain.

PEA PLANTER
This tractor is pulling a pea-planting machine, which levels the soil, drills holes, and plants the seeds. It takes its power from the tractor.

PRINTING

COPYING A LETTER OR A BOOK WAS A LONG AND difficult job before printing was invented. A person called a scribe made every copy by hand. The invention of printing and copying machines allowed many copies to be made very easily.

CHINESE PRINT BLOCK
More than 3,000 years ago, the Chinese were printing with carved stone or wood blocks.

The first printing process was called letterpress printing. Pictures or words were carved into wood. The blocks were inked and pressed on to paper. Later metal letters called type were put together to make words. The photocopier made copying documents much more convenient. The photocopier was invented in 1938 by American law student Chester Carlson. It used light and **static electricity** to produce a copy.

Paper loading tray

Feed rollers

MODERN PRINTING
This book was printed on a machine like the one shown here. The four colors that make up all the others are printed in turn. It can print over 10,000 sheets of paper an hour.

Lens

COPY

Each sheet of paper is moved through the machine on rollers. A copy of the original document is fed out at the top.

Exposure lamps

Paper transport rollers

Mirror

DRUM CHARGER

At the start of the copying cycle, the drum is charged with static electricity by the drum charger.

Cleaning brush

FUSER

The heater warms the paper. This softens the toner, making it fuse onto the paper. This is why paper is warm when it comes out of a photocopier.

DRUM

The rotating drum is the heart of the machine. Light from the document shines on to the drum via mirrors and lenses. The more charge that the drum contains, the darker the printed document.

Toner

TONER FEED BELT

The toner brush puts toner, a colored powder, on the drum. The toner sticks to areas that are still charged, printing a copy of the original.

TELEPHONE

Two inventors patented the telephone on the same day in 1876. They were Alexander Graham Bell (see page 21) and Elisha Gray (1835–1901). They both worked out how to make a microphone, which allowed sound to be sent along a wire. Bell formed the Bell Telephone Company in 1877.

The first telephone systems had just two telephones, with a wire between them. Two years later the first telephone exchange opened in New Haven, Connecticut. Gradually exchanges were linked together, forming the first telephone **networks**. The first hand-held cell phone was developed in 1973 by Motorola. The first **cellular** telephone networks opened the following year. Since then handsets have become smaller and more complex, and the networks can now carry pictures and digital data, as well as sound.

CENTRAL PROCESSOR

The processor controls the phone by carrying out programmed instructions. The instructions are stored in the phone's memory.

THE FIRST PHONE

This is a copy of Alexander Graham Bell's telephone of 1876. The tube on the left was both the mouthpiece and earpiece. The central section turned sound into electricity and back again.

CAMERA

This is a camera phone. It has a small lens with a light-sensitive microchip behind. Images and video are stored in the phone's memory and can be sent to other phones.

BATTERY

A rechargeable battery powers the antenna that sends radio signals to the network.

SCREEN

The display is a high-resolution, liquid-crystal, thin-film transistor (TFT), color screen. It is used to show the phone's menus, photographs, video, and information, such as battery life.

SWITCHBOARDS

The first telephone exchanges were operated by hand. Modern exchanges are digital and are part of a huge communications network.

Earphone

Vibrator unit

Camera button

Joystick

SIM CARD

The subscriber information module (SIM) stores the information the phone needs to connect to its network, and also the user's phone numbers.

Keypad

TELESCOPE

A TELESCOPE IS AN INSTRUMENT THAT MAKES distant objects look larger. The first telescopes were made in the early 1600s. Soon, astronomers were using the new instrument to discover new planets and stars in the Universe.

NEBULA BY HUBBLE
This image was taken by Hubble *in 1995. It shows giant columns of gas and dust in the Eagle Nebula, 7,000* **light years** *from Earth.*

Nobody is sure who made the first telescope. However, we do know that Hans Lippershey (see page 23) made telescopes that used lenses. The reflecting telescope, which uses mirrors, was invented by the English physicist Sir Isaac Newton (1642–1727). Swirling air currents in the atmosphere alter the view through telescopes. In 1990 this problem was solved by the launch of the *Hubble* Space Telescope. *Hubble* gives us incredibly clear views of the universe from space. Some telescopes on Earth receive clear images by using computers to remove any distortions.

APERTURE
Light enters the telescope here. The door is closed when the telescope is not in use.

Aperture door

HARLAN J. SMITH TELESCOPE
Paving the way for the space-age Hubble, *this $5 million telescope weighs over 3 tons and has a primary mirror measuring almost 9 feet in diameter.*

HUBBLE SPACE
TELESCOPE
HUBBLE'S *HUGE MIRRORS*
CAN "SEE" *AN OBJECT THE*
SIZE OF A PERSON
2,500 MILES AWAY.

Hans Lippershey (1570-1619) worked *making eye glasses in the Netherlands. It is likely that he put two lenses in front of each other and saw a magnified image. He used this effect to build the first telescope.*

MAIN MIRROR

The primary mirror is nearly 8 feet across. It collects light and reflects it on to the secondary mirror. This reflects the light on to the instruments.

Secondary mirror

Antenna

SOLAR CELLS

Two 39-foot solar panels convert sunlight into the electricity *Hubble* needs to work. Spare electricity is stored in batteries for use when *Hubble* is in shade.

MAIN COMPUTERS

One computer controls the instruments and transmits a signal to the ground. The other operates the pointing control system.

STIS

NICMOS

Support frame

Gyroscopes

WFPC

Batteries

GUIDANCE SYSTEM

The pointing control system aims *Hubble* accurately at objects in space. There are sensors that check the direction and **actuators**, which tilt the telescope.

SCIENTIFIC INSTRUMENTS

Hubble has four main instruments. They are the Advanced Camera for Surveys (ACS, shown here), the Near Infrared Camera and Multi-Object Spectrometer (NICMOS), the Space Telescope Imaging Spectrograph (STIS), and the Wide Field and Planetary Camera (WFPC).

BARLOW'S SPUR MOTOR
British physicist Peter Barlow (1776–1862) demonstrated this motor in 1822. Electricity flowing in the wheel between the magnets made the wheel turn.

CHUCK

The drill bit is held firmly by the chuck. Tightening the chuck presses metal jaws on to the bit. This chuck is tightened by a key.

Drive shaft

Drill bit

Grip

An electric motor works using electromagnets. Danish physicist Hans Christian Oersted (1777–1851) discovered **electromagnetism** in 1820. He saw that a compass needle moved when the electricity in a nearby wire was switched on. The next year Michael Faraday (see page 25) invented an electric motor. A simple electric motor has two main parts. In the center are coils of wire on a rotor. Around it are fixed magnets. An electric current in the coils turns them into magnets. They attract and repel the fixed magnets, making the rotor spin.

ELECTRIC CAR
The experimental Eliica car is powered by electric motors. Electricity for the motors comes from rechargeable batteries. Eliica weighs 2.5 tons, but is faster than most sports cars. Its top speed is an incredible 230 mph.

POWER DRILL
THE FIRST ELECTRIC
HAND DRILL WAS
BUILT IN 1895 BY A
GERMAN INVENTOR
NAMED WILHELN FEIN.

Michael Faraday (1791–1867) was a
British physicist. He made important
discoveries about electricity and
magnetism. He built the first working
electric motor and invented the
electricity generator.

Speed setting switch

ELECTRIC MOTOR

The motor in a drill is
called a universal motor.
Electricity travels to the
coils of wire in the rotor
through a pair of contacts,
called a commutator.

Commutator

Brushes

Magnets

Copper coils

Fan

Plastic
casing

GEARS

Gears transfer
power from the
motor to the chuck.
They reduce the
speed that the chuck
turns, but increase
the turning power.

SWITCH

The switch turns the
motor on and off. It also
controls the flow of the
electricity, making the
motor turn slowly or fast.

Insulation

Power
cable

Chuck key

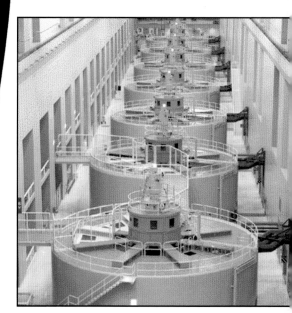

GENERATORS

*An electricity generator
does the reverse job of a
motor, turning movement
into electricity. These
generators are inside a
hydroelectric power station,
where water movement is
converted into electricity.*

CAMERA

THE INVENTION OF THE MOVIE CAMERA BEGAN THE movie industry. Movie cameras record moving images onto strips of film. They were the only way to record movies until video recording was invented in the 1950s.

EARLY PHOTOGRAPHY
People in early photographs had to keep very still for up to eight minutes. This is why they were often pictured sitting down. Movement made the image blur.

In 1827 French inventor Joseph Niepce (1765–1833) took the first-ever photograph. It was recorded on a metal plate coated with light-sensitive chemicals. Moving photographs became possible in the 1880s, when film became good enough to record a photograph in a split second. Then, American inventor Thomas Edison (1847–1931) built the first movie camera. The Lumières (see page 27) used a similar machine to record movies. Electronic television cameras were developed in the 1920s, but their pictures could not be recorded until the 1950s. Video cameras were developed in the 1970s and digital video cameras in the 1980s.

HIGH-DEFINITION VIDEO
State-of-the-art video cameras record digital high-definition video. Film makers are using them instead of film cameras.

French brothers Auguste (1862–1954) and Louis Lumière (1864–1948) opened the world's first movie theater in Paris in 1895.

FEED SPOOL
This holds the reel of film before it has been exposed.

Film

Handle

Take-up spool

Light-proof box

Camera rear door

GATE
The film moves down through the gate. It stops briefly for a frame to be recorded on it, then moves to the next frame.

SHUTTER
The shutter opens when the film is stopped in the gate. This lets light hit the film and record a frame.

LENS
The lens gathers light from the scene. It bends the light and focuses it on to the film in the gate.

CLAW
The claw is a mechanism that pulls the film down through the gate one frame at a time. Throughout the silent movie era, the claw pulled through 16 frames per second.

CAM
The cam is an egg-shaped wheel. As it turns round the "bump" pushes the claw up and down.

COMPUTER

THE COMPUTER IS PROBABLY THE MOST USEFUL machine ever invented. It can perform almost any job we program it to do. For example, we use computers for sending e-mails, writing, and looking at photographs. Computers also fly aircraft, help diagnose illnesses, and work games consoles.

In the 1880s, Charles Babbage (see below) designed a mechanical computer. The first electric computers were built in the 1940s. They took up whole rooms, but were less powerful than modern-day calculators. After the transistor was invented in 1948, computers became faster, cheaper, and more reliable. The integrated circuit (microchip) was invented in 1958. This allowed complex circuits to be squeezed into a tiny space. The first microprocessor chip was launched in 1972, and the first personal computers were developed soon afterward. The first version of Microsoft Windows™ appeared in 1985.

BABBAGE'S MACHINE
This is a modern model of a calculating machine designed in the 1820s by Charles Babbage (1792–1871). It was too complicated to build at the time.

KEYBOARD
The keyboard is for typing text and numbers into the computer. It is also used for controlling the computer.

MONITOR
The monitor displays text, images, video, and other information held on the computer.

MOUSE
The mouse controls the position of a pointer on the screen. The pointer is used to choose things on the screen. The mouse uses either motion-sensitive wheels, or a light, to detect movement.

Konrad Zuse (1910–95) built the first computer that could be programmed in 1941. It was called Z3. He also invented one of the first computer languages. He used the language to write the first chess-playing program.

OPTICAL DRIVE

The optical drive reads and writes information on CD-ROM and DVD discs.

CENTRAL PROCESSING UNIT

The CPU is the computer's "brain." It sorts out information and controls all the other computer parts.

POWER SUPPLY

The power supply provides electricity for the circuits, hard drive motors, and cooling fans.

MOTHERBOARD

All the computer's electronic circuits are attached to the motherboard. The main microchip on the board is called the processor.

Fan

HARD DRIVE

The hard drive stores programs and information. They are saved even when the computer is turned off.

Video card

Sound card

Modem card

MEMORY BOARD

Programs and information are loaded in the computer's memory when it is turned on. The memory is called random access memory (RAM).

Speaker

GLOSSARY

actuator
Device that makes part of a machine move

aviator
Person who flies aircraft

avionics
Electronic circuits that help a pilot to fly and navigate an aircraft

cellular
A telephone network used for cell phones

combustion
Another word for burning

commutator
Device that changes the flow of electricity

computer language
Instructions written in a language that a computer can understand

diesel engine
Internal combustion engine that uses an oil, called diesel oil, as its fuel

electromagnetism
When an electric current creates a magnet, or a moving magnet creates an electric current

ethyl alcohol
Liquid often used as a fuel, made from sugar

exhaust
Gases that come out of an engine

gas engine
Internal combustion engine that uses gases as its fuel

gasoline engine
Internal combustion engine that uses a liquid called gasoline as its fuel

gears
Sets of toothed wheels that allow an engine to turn a vehicle's wheels at different speeds

glider
Aircraft without an engine, which gains height by flying in rising air currents, or by being towed by another aircraft

gyroscope
Navigation device with a heavy spinning flywheel inside. The wheel always stays at the same angle.

internal combustion engine
Engine in which the fuel burns in spaces inside the engine, such as the diesel engine and gasoline engine

kilobyte
Measure of computer memory

light year
Distance that light travels in a year, which is about 5.88 trillion miles

liquid oxygen
Oxgyen that is cooled and pressurised to turn it into liquid

locomotive
Machine that pulls or pushes railroad cars

mass production
Making objects in large quantities, normally on a production line, where pieces are added to the objects as they move through a factory

navigate
To find the way from place to place

nebula
Giant cloud of gas and dust in space

network
Pathways that connect things together, such as the links between telephones

pneumatic
Using air or other gases to work, such as an air-filled tire

radar
Device that detects objects in the air by sending out radio waves and detecting any waves that bounce back

self-propelled
Vehicle with an engine that moves along under its own power

stabilator
In aircraft, a combined elevator (which controls the up-and-down movement of the nose) and horizontal stabilizer (which helps the aircraft to balance)

static electricity
Electricity that clings to an object's surface, rather than flowing through it

thrust
Push made by a jet engine

turbofan
Type of jet engine used by most modern jet aircraft

vacuum
Space almost without any sort of gas

INDEX